Universal You

Crystals & Precious Gemstones

"Manipura"

Solar Plexus Chakra Energy
Centre Complementary Crystals

Author, Illustrator & Photographer : M- J -Summers

Content

From the Author

The Solar Plexus chakra, crystal complementary guide was created to bring you a greater understanding of the metaphysical healing uses and purposes of individual crystals. Crystals encompass and enhance an array of magnificent positive energies, that will assist you on your spiritual journey. Crystals can help to create inner alignment, balance, bliss, harmony, a sense of security and peace, while strengthening the inner and outer energy connection to one's Mind, Body & Spirit, as well as many other benefits.

Daily practice with crystals will assist you with protection and clearing blockages of negative energies, turning them into positive new fierce forces. Crystals can also give aid with raising natural vibration higher, as well as your awareness. Crystals therefore will assist in one's spiritual advancement, when one wishes to attain optimal energy levels within and connect to the collective consciousness of unconditional love and oneness..

Acknowledgements

I would like to express my greatest gratitude, to all souls that have collectively supported me along my journey. From my "Family" & "Soul Friends" and all other souls I have encountered, at the many crossroads on my evolutionary journey throughout this life.

I would like to dedicate this book especially to my little SisStar - "Kerry". This includes all my other soul siblings, Brothers' & SisStars' alike.

I would like to give a huge "thank you" firstly, to my little SisStar - Kerry, for teaching me so many lessons while on our journey together. Thank you for choosing to share this lifetime with me. I love you unconditionally and eternally. I promise to eternally watch over you, protect you, and love you as big SisStars do.

To my best friend also, who is just alike my big SisStar - Karen Aka - "Mary" & whom goes by many other titles. Thank you for every single shared memory, and all the giggles gained along the path. Patsy, may we continue to have much more fun & create more magical memories, as we share this continued journey together.

To my other soul SisStars, Vicky, Joyce, Cassie, Gina, Kathrine, Gemma, Louisa Aka - "Luby Lou", Tamara, Josephine & Zoe – Aka "Mrs B" or "Rosey Lee". Thank you, ladies of lovelight, for your continued support and unconditional love along the way.

This book is also dedicated to my soul Brothers – Stuart, Jason, Dave & Tommy. I am eternally grateful for everything you guys have ever done to support me, guide me, teach me. Just being there as my Little Brothers. Although, on some occasions', you may have had to act as my BIG Brothers, "Thank you". To John for all your technical support. I AM truly grateful for each of your souls'. To both my SisStars and Brothers, I AM infinitely grateful for what you have each done along the way to protect, nurture, and encourage my growth, as well as my Children's. Infinite light and eternal love – Michelle - oxo MJ –

A special thank you to my other soul Brother Callum, for always being there for me. You are one of the best seeds source could have ever sent me "Thank you". I am grateful beyond words to have served you and to have been served by you, and I will always remind you of how grateful I am! So much Love & Light MJ. oxoxo

I give thanks alike, for all other Soul Brothers and Sisters along this path, that have come into my life along the way, and that have left too. I am respectfully thankful to each of you, as you have all contributed to my lessons, blessings, and growth. I am thankful for you all un-conditionally. MJ. oxoxo

Thanks also to Stuart Naples –AKA - "Billy" for your friendship time and efforts given to my-self and Universal you. oxoxo

Gratitude "Namaste".

I would also like to acknowledge and give greatest thanks to, "Source Creator to the highest and our entire Universe".

I AM truly grateful for all the lessons I have been taught in all lifetimes, and especially while building this book. I AM super thankful that I've been able to grow in such light and love, so that even in my darkest lessons within life, I was able to transform these lessons and energies into blessings. Lessons and blessings in life that we can all share collectively. So that we are able to teach each other in return, as we all grow into, and as ONE.

Additionally, I give thanks all the beautiful Souls' reading this book right now, and making a difference in the World energetically. I give thanks and respect to all the, "free thinkers" of this World who seek "The Truth".

We are all "Energy".
Magnetic, Manifesting Magicians" Collectively we are free. Infinite Love & Light – Mj oxox

Introduction

Crystals are minerals, formed underground from three-dimensional repeating patterns of atoms. A crystal's appearance depends upon the natural characteristics of its category, and the conditions in which it grows. Specific ones take on strange shapes, some are very small, and others grow very large, developing over thousands and millions of years.

The repeating chemical structure of crystals, is said to empower them with a "sort of memory". This means that crystals have the power to hold energies. You can also hold a Quartz crystal with the intention of filling it with your love or desires. This is what is meant by encoding or coding a crystal. You do not need any a special connection or wires. All you need to practice the energy alchemy of crystals, is a little faith, and inner will, as well attention and intention.

The crystal will therefore remember your love, which will then penetrate all environments in which the crystal is placed. Crystals can remember negative, as well as positive energies, and therefore will need to be cleansed regularly. Its known if you place an amethyst in a certain room, it will help to cleanse a room of negative energies. This means the Amethyst then absorbed an element of the negative energies, and will require cleansing alike.

Single terminated wands

These have a single point at one end, and a rough or rounded edge at the other. They are used widely in cleansing, healing, jewellery and meditation.

Chunks

Chunks are crystals without notable facets. They can be good for enriching a rooms atmosphere, for body layouts, felicitating meditation, grids, rituals, or for carrying on your person, in pockets or purses.

Clusters

Clusters consist of a group of small crystals that have naturally grown and joined together. Clusters can be excellent for enriching a living environment or workplace. Depending upon their properties, they can cleanse, calm, invigorate or purify the atmosphere.

Cut crystals

Crystals that have been cut and polished into shapes such as pyramids, spheres or wands, thus making them appear very attractive. If they are well-cut, the energy of the stone can be maintained and sometimes amplified.

Tumble stones

Tumble stones are small stones, rocks, or crystals that have been tumbled over each other many times, with an increasingly finer abrasive motion until the sides become smooth and shiny. Many people like to carry a crystal tumble stone around in their pocket, to keep the energy of the stone in their presence always.

You do not need to know the exact properties of every stone to buy one. Although, it is more important to be receptive and allow yourself to be drawn to a specific stone. That way it will hold a precise meaning for you. If you are in a crystal shop, you can stand in front of some selected crystals, close your eyes and relax, and when you open them, choose the one you feel most drawn to.

You may find yourself drawn to a specific crystal with a powerful urge to touch and feel it. If you feel that you very much want that crystal to be a part of your life, it is likely that on some level it has something to offer you and your personal growth. As with all purchases relating to spiritual growth intent is crucial, and you may need to acknowledge that the time isn't right. If you buy crystals purely because that is what you set out to do that day, then your crystals may lack meaning and you are fundamentally starting a rock collection.

Secured with the knowledge of where the imbalances and blockages are located, crystal healers use a wide variety of techniques and layouts to channel "Universal Life Force", to the affected chakra energy centre, which can be located generally by the colour of stone. Some use the power within the stone, others use the crystals as conduits and amplifiers of their own healing powers. Both approaches can be very beneficial.

Laying on of stones

Laying on of stones involves using the natural life force found in the crystals, to affect the re balancing of the chakra, by placing the crystals on or near the chakra. Then leaving them there for a certain time period to affect the re- balancing and un-blocking of energies. Again, while there are many patterns and layouts that can be used, a simple application of a suitable crystal to the chakra area, for a 5-10-minute period can be very effective. Sometimes, a simple approach always works best. Although it might not be best in all cases, the simple "laying on of stones", has been found to be highly effective for countless healers. Since it is a "self-help method" it is one approach anyone can practice and refine.

Crystals complementary to our chakra energy centres

Chakras are made up of a networking system of energy. The seven major chakras are found along the subtle body in alignment with the shaft of the spine. The seven chakras centres are the energy pools of spiritual power within the human body, that connect your mind, body and soul to the Heavens and the Earth.

The lower chakras are associated with the fundamental aspects in our lives, such as our emotions and needs, here on Earth. Earth vibrates at a lower frequency. Therefore, is denser in its nature. The upper energies of one's chakra system, is correspond to the higher aspects of our mental and spiritual connection, aspirations and services.

Each chakra is associated with a certain part of the body and a specific organ, which provides each organ with the energies it needs. In-order for one's energies to function and flow correctly. In addition to this, just as every organ has a counterpart on the mental and spiritual level, each chakra communicates and corresponds to a specific aspect of our human behaviours and our development.

For us to evolve and become fully self-conscious and at peace with our physical and spiritual nature, our denser lower energies need to be harmonized. One can attain this with the higher lighter energies of the upper centres. One must be prepared to raise the survival base tendencies within, in order to incorporate a purer, heart-felt spiritual focus of universal oneness and love, un-conditionally, allowing us to fully and freely express all areas of our being within. Each of the upper-level energies corresponds and refines a lower level counterpart: 7th with 1st, 6th with 2nd, 5th with 3rd. In the centre of our being the 4th it fully integrates all into the heart.

In attaining the wisdom of our subtle energy systems, thus empowers us to maintain balance and harmony on the physical, mental and spiritual levels. All meditation reiki and yoga practices, seek to balance out the energy within the chakras, by purifying the lower energies and guiding them upwards. This can be achieved by creating your internal sacred space, and grounding your energies daily. Furthermore, by living consciously with an awareness of how we acquire and exhaust our energy. When we become mindful of these energy exchanges, we then become capable of balancing our life force with our mental, physical and spiritual selves to attain alignment. Although crystal energies can vary, they can be used to balance and align the chakra energy centres.

How to know when your Solar Plexus Chakra energy centre, is aligned or is un-balanced?

When imbalances occur in a person's Solar Plexus Chakra, they might show signs of having various abdominal problems, lower back pain, digestive problems, and respiratory problems. A person may also suffer from skin disease s or disorders, and diabetes. One can also exhibit signs of having arthritis, cardio vascular disease and gout. There is a catalogue of issues that can occur, when ones Solar Plexus energy center is blocked, or stagnate. A person with a blocked Manipura chakra center, might also portray signs of becoming very fearful, and fear emotions such as criticism, failure, and rejection. They can also become very ill, and develop a strong fear of death and dying.

The goal in balancing this chakra, is to work on a balanced diet. Try to eat healthier, by becoming aware of the food products that hold low vibrations, and by also avoiding them. Therefore, trying to be mindful to consume more foods that contain stronger vibrations. These higher frequency foods are rich in nutrients, for example: greens like, beans, broccoli and watercress any green root foods. Furthermore, there are other high frequency food sources, like berries, fruits, grains, herbs and nuts. Become more physical and do more exercise. Even if it means doing work in your garden, get outdoors and back into nature.

When a balance in the Manipura occurs between Prana and Apana, they become united and guided to the "Sushuma Nadi "CNS" Aka - The central nervous system. When this occurs, the Kundalini, energy rises to the Sahasrara chakra, the "Crown" chakra, and then one can experience the state of bliss, and supreme consciousness of "Oneness".

Combining the uses of individual Crystals and the complimentary energies they herald, will amplify, enhance, and transform your present energies onto a higher frequency of vibration and being.

Cleansing & Charging Your Crystals'

Often people prefer to cleanse their crystals after purchase, prior to using them for the first time. Whether it be cleansing a newly sought stone, or if it's just time to refresh your crystals energies. In-order to clear any negative energies that they have collected. This chapter will guide you to a greater understanding of just how to cleanse your precious crystals and gemstones......

There are a few exclusions from the crystal families that never have to be "recharged", such as Quartz from Nepal and Tibet. Furthermore, there are crystals that hold ancient knowledge and wisdoms and are full of energy and histories that are simply magical.

Why should you cleanse your crystals?

Recharging your crystals restores them back to their original state, as well as the vibrant vibrational levels to where they can do their best work. Assisting and supporting you. Understand, everything is made up from energy, and absolutely everything has a vibration. This includes emotions and physical objects, such as crystals.

Negative energies, such as negative emotions and physical pain, have low vibrations. Crystals, when they are at their purest most optimal vibrational state, resonate at an extremely high vibration. Low and high vibrations cannot exist together.

The crystals will help one to raise and transform, any low energies to higher ones. Complementary to adding additional high vibrational energies to one's person or immediate environment, thus having magnificent benefits to one's overall health and well-being is increased. Crystals that you work with, or keep on your person often, should be cleansed more regularly than the ones that may simply be sitting around, or in a box somewhere.

However, it is nice to give all your precious gems an energetic boost too at times. One may simply use their intuition on how often to cleanse and purify one's crystals.

Cleansing Methods

Crystals- Druzy, Bed, Geode or Cluster

All crystals can be cleansed safely by placing them inside an Amethyst geode cave overnight or for 24-48 hours. An Amethyst druzy, cluster, or bed can also be used in the same way. A clear Quartz geode bed or clusters provides a faster cleansing process than Amethyst. Although both methods are equally as effective. Simply place no more than a few crystals onto the crystal points, and leave for anything up to 24-48 hours.

These crystal clusters formations, both Amethyst and Quartz, can absorb the energies contained within crystals. Therefore, neutralising the energies and then release 'good' energy from the clusters back into the crystals being cleansed. They can effectively cleanse and energize at the same time.

Additional cleansing complimentary crystals are: Carnelian clusters. Citrine clusters, Rose Quartz clusters and Selenite clusters.

Crystal Singing Bowl / Non-Contact Salt

Crystal tuner - Singing bowls are tuned to specific frequencies found within the human body. When the sound transports through the atmosphere and touches us, it causes our cells to move in different directions at a different speed, in rhythm with the sound wave that has been absorbed. Additionally, crystals have been shown to oscillate at their own frequencies, and even respond to the input of vibrations. Therefore, when we come into contact with a crystal, its vibration interacts with the vibration of the cells in our body and vice versa. The bowls-tuners can also be used to cleanse one's crystal collection as-well as one's energy aura.

Salt- Cleaning is considered the safest method, and can be used if the crystals otherwise are not damaged, or have become damaged by direct contact with salt. This is also a good method if you are cleansing gemstones in jewellery, or gems encased in metals.

Firstly, fill a glass bowl half to two thirds full of dry sea salt, cooking salt or grinded sea salt. Then place a smaller glass container, or shallow drinking glass, and half-bury this into the salt. You can then place your crystals directly into the empty glass, which is sitting half buried in the dry salt.

The salt will still be able to draw out the stored energies within the stones, but this method will take longer to work than direct contact with salt. You may also pour just enough water, preferably pure distilled or mineral water, into the smaller glass container, just enough to cover the crystals. This will protect them, preventing direct salt exposure or salty air, causing any corrosion or adverse effects to any metals, or other fittings that may surround the gems. Also, bear in mind that certain crystals should not be left to soak in water or direct salts.

Then afterwards, the used salt should be thrown away and never re-used, as it holds all the negative energies it's just extracted from the crystals.

Earth Burial

You may also choose to bury your stone in the Earth. But again, make sure that you know if the stone is one that can take being bathed in water, in case rain seeps through to where the stone is being stored to recharge.

You can bury them in the Earth for 1 day to a week. Either in your garden, or in a flower pot. Proceed with caution and be sure, that if you bury your crystals in the garden, that you mark the spot. You don't want to have to dig up half the garden to find your stones again. Otherwise protect them well while recharging the stones.

Moonlight & Sunlight

The moonlight and sunlight, herald a powerful influence that will re-energize your crystals, and allow them to lift their vibration naturally. Therefore, this being the prime time for cleansing crystals. Additionally, at the time of a full moon, when it is at its greatest illumination, its energy is strongest. If you wish, you can combine the use of moonlight charging along with other above suggested methods for cleansing your crystals and your precious stones. Your crystals and gemstones will become charged and more vibrant and next time you use them. They will be ready to serve you to the fullest. They don't need to be left out-doors in the moonlight or sunlight to absorb the positive energy, but it can be an added advantage if you are able to place them somewhere in your home, like your "window ledge", where they will be in direct contact with the moonlight or sunlight for as long as possible. Leave them there all-day or overnight. If you can. By absorbing the energy of moonlight or sunlight, you will allow their vibration to naturally lift. Proceed forth with caution, when placing them in areas directly exposed to strong sunlight for long periods of time, as this can damage and ultimately cause discolouring within them. When losing their attractive and distinctive colours may not have a direct effect on their energy, you may feel frustrated or dissatisfied, if they are no longer the colour they once were when you acquired them. Some additional stones that are not to be in cleansed in the Sun-light are: Amethyst, Ametrine, Celestite, Fluorite, Green Apophyllite, Opal, Prestolite, Rose Quartz, Smokey Quartz, Super Seven, Topaz and Turquoise.

If you have any uncertainties at all, be sure to do your research on your collection of crystals and only use only moonlight cleansing.

Rice Cleansing

You can use any type of rice for cleaning your crystals. Either brown or white rice, and it's very easy to do. You can use rice cleansing if you are wary of using water or sage, and this may be especially helpful if you have a gemstone that is very rare, or indeed precious to you. Simply place your stones on top of the rice and leave overnight. This method is very easy and simple, yet very effective indeed. The rice will naturally absorb negative energies. So, you will need to throw it out after using it, alike the used salt as stated before. Crystal size depending, you may choose to cover it with rice, or simply place it on top of the rice. Again, one can ultimately use their intuition to guide and determine, what is the best cleansing method for your precious gemstones and just how you should choose to cleanse and re-charge them individually. Understand that one specific cleansing method might suit a one stone better than another, and these are stated in the chapters ahead.

Salt Water

Although this is a widespread way to clear crystals, I recommend using salt water very carefully, if at all. You must understand, and fully know all about your crystals so to be sure that they are not porous or soft, so they won't be damaged by the salt-water. Salt-water can steep into the structures of some crystals and stones, which can cause irreparable damage and ultimately, over time, causing them to break. Some stones that are not to be cleansed in salt water are: Alabaster, Amethyst, Calcite, Carnelian, Halite, Hematite,

Labradorite/Spectrolite, Lepidolite, Lodestone
"Magnetite", Mica, Moldavite, Opal, Turquoise,
Ulexite, All clusters of most crystals. Remain mindful
that when you do use salt water, do so cautiously.
Don't leave your crystals in salt - water longer than
absolutely necessary.

Some additional stones that are not to be cleansed in
Water are: Adamite, Azurite, Desert Rose, Fibrous,
Garnets, Malachite, Fulgurite, Halite, Rock Salt,
Selenite, Sulphur, Vanadalite, Vanadinite and
Wavellite.
Cleaning your crystals with water is NOT
recommended, unless you know about whether your
stone is safe to cleanse this way. Please take care
when using water on large delicate clusters, as they can
still be damaged by water, so please do take care with
your crystals.

Smudging

Crystals can be cleansed by smudging them. This exercise is so easy. So how do you smudge your crystals? The most effective smudge tool to use is white sage. It is possible to buy smudge sticks readymade, but I prefer to grow and dry my own Sage to use. Often smudge sticks are made up of either white sage alone or mixed with lavender. Again, you can cultivate your own herbs and mix and match, when you create your own at home. Many may use other fragrant herbs in their bundles as well, and some of them may also have healing properties that will benefit you, as well give a fresh neutralising fragrance to combat the energies surrounding one in the Air. Sage smoke is a powerful cleansing tool, for both you and your stones, and the environment where they are placed. To cleanse your crystal, you can hold the stones close to the flow of the smoke or simply hold your smudge stick near to where they are placed. So, the air around them is full of the sage essence. This is the method most alchemical healers use, to quickly cleanse their stones and crystal wands after use within healings, rituals or works

White Light "Thought & Visualisation"

There are many different methods for cleansing natural crystals of various varieties and types. Simply by using white light. This is a powerful method, once you know how to create it. Most of you have the capacity to create white light, and this may also be called divine white light or universal light. Another alternative to using white light, is candle light. The flame of a candle can be used, along with one's intention to cleanse and purify your crystals.

The first time you do it close your eyes, and ask Almighty Source Creator, Universe, Spirit. Whatever you believe in to be the creator to support you, by allowing you to create divine white light. This works alike the precious power of prayer.

Imagine your body filling up with the white light, coming in through your Crown chakra and then feel it add to the energy that you have already within you. Open your eyes and direct the white light to your chosen crystals. Meanwhile, using your hands in a small

31

circular, sweeping motion, towards where you want to direct the energy of the white light.

Ask the universe to use the white light to transmute any negative energy within the stone into positive energy. Not only can this method be used for cleansing crystals, the white divine light can also be used on yourself and others to heal, as well as contribute to raising your vibration.

Furthermore, this divine white light can be used to improve the energy of a room, space or your immediate environment. I cleanse my stones often. This is extremely important if you are using them as tools daily within meditation. White light is the easiest and most effective method to remove any built-up negative energy quickly.

Certain crystals do not require cleansing, a brief list of some of these crystals are: Amethyst, Citrine, Diamond, Fulgurite, Herkimer Diamond and Super Seven.

Gold

 Gold symbolises the purity within the spiritual aspect of, "All That Is". It is highly symbolic of spirituality and development within the realm of complete understanding. Therefore, allowing one to both attain and maintain communion with the source of all being. Gold has been called "the master healer". It is an excellent mineral for purification of the physical body.

Gold was discovered approximately 3000 B. C.

Gold has been mined in many locations world-wide, from Australia, California, Japan, Nevada, Papa New Guinea, Peru, and South Africa.

Astrologically, Gold's energies are said to complement the zodiac birth signs of Leo. Gold energies are alike the energy elements of the fire and sun in nature.

Historically, Gold's been located worldwide, but over 40% of the worlds Gold is mined in Witwatersrand basin in South Africa. Its recognised as the richest Gold fields to ever be discovered. It's also recorded, that in the 1970's South Africa's output of Gold was a79% contribution to the overall amount accounted for world-wide.

Metaphysically, Gold enhances one's sense of balance. The balancing effects it projects expands on all levels of the mind, body and soul. This will enhance and support the wearer with healing energies, as it will boost and balance our overall combined energies of the mind, body and soul, allowing one to receive freely, a greater flow of healing energy. Gold compliments and stimulates one's masculine energies.

Uses and Purposes

Gold produces an energy which is both harmonious and receptive, allowing an expanded use with other gemstones. Gold can attract and maintaining those qualities / energies, which are inherent within the additional stone. When in proximity to another mineral, gold provides a stabilising influence to the energies of that mineral.

Gold is a super conductor, and is used within computer chips to produce circuits.

Gold nanoparticles are increasingly being used as industrial catalysts. Vinyl acetate, which is used to make PVA for glues, paints, and resins are made using Gold catalyst.

Gold is often used within decoration, for purposes such as architectural art, coins, jewellery and ornamental objects.

Mind, Body & Soul Healing Therapies

__Emotional Healing Energy__ - Gold has been said to attract wealth and happiness. Gold can provide energies that will compose, balance and stabilise the emotional system, so to relieve one's mind, body, and soul from tension and stress.

Gold can both amplify positive feelings, and assists one with attuning into nature, and all of nature's healing forces. Gold has a balancing and harmonizing effect on all levels of body, mind, and spirit. It is used to enhance and improve mental attitude and emotional states. It has also been reported to promote a feeling of increased energy within the bearer.

Gold supports and strengthens our will power, mental focus, and is known to stimulate the libido. Gold helps to improve one's growth via learning, and lessening the traumas associated with situations that one might have experienced during life's lessons, and attainment of knowledge.

The energy of gold itself, can be used to balance the surrounding energy fields and to assist one in the elimination of ego conflicts and uneasy feelings. It can also help to assist with decreasing the energy feeling one may have of overburden and responsibility. Gold is also used to combat feelings of depression and inferiority, to allow one to understand, and transmute any feelings of anger.

Physical Healing Energy – Gold is said to be a regenerator, supporting one to renew oneself as it works on all levels of the physical, mental, and spiritual planes encompassing all. It is proposed that gold will benefit the nervous system, and improve the ability of the nerves function, to transmit information in the most efficient style.

Gold will aid the digestion system by harmonizing the energies, and this allows one to harness the knowledge and understanding of proper consumption of food. Therefore, this benefits the circulatory system, as well as assisting one to detoxify the blood.

Gold is said to increase the ability for the body to exchange oxygen from the lungs into the blood, by amplify strength, this will sharpen our mental focus towards the positive aspects of our lives, and boost our self-confidence as well as improve the quality of our life.

Gold is also said to be of great importance to individuals with arthritis or heart disease, or because it supports the body to rid its self of blockages. Additionally, according to studies, Colloidal Gold will increase mental ability and activity, as well as enhance one's concentration. Colloidal Gold is thought to strengthen mental function by increasing the conductivity between nerve endings in the brain, and body.

Gold has additionally been used within healing therapies as an aid or a cure in some cases, for people suffering from arthritis.

Gold has additionally been used to enhance mental faculties, to rebuild the nervous system. Gold alloy is also used by dentists in fillings.

Chakra Healing Energy ~ Gold is predominately of similar energies to the Solar Plexus, but it has also been used to open, and to activate the third-eye and crown chakras, as the purity of gold is said to help one to preserve higher thought forms and connection spiritually.

Gold can also boost and attract positive energies to the wearer, as well as assist to un-block any blockages within the solar plexus chakra centre.

Gold can clear negativity from the chakras, and the energy fields of the physical, intellectual, emotional, and spiritual bodies, while transmuting vitality from all companion minerals to the Solar Plexus chakra, or the specific affected area in need of healing, cleansing, and balancing. Additionally, Gold has also been used in the purification, development, and balancing of the heart chakra.

<u>Activating, Charging, Cleansing & Purifying methods</u>
<u>for your Gold.</u> Gold can be charged and cleansed by
reiki, the sun, sage, and water. Although, moon-light
and smudging are the safest options for cleansing all
your precious crystals and gemstones.

Heliodor

 Heliodor is considered as a gift of the sun, to the earth. Heliodor is a bright yellow crystal, that is regarded as the crystal containing the warmth and brightness of the sunshine. Heliodor also belongs to the mineral class of beryllium aluminium silicate. Many other crystals belong to the Beryl family, such as Aquamarine, Emerald, Goshenite, Morganite, and red Beryl. Heliodor can often be mistaken for as yellow Topaz, because Heliodor colour is often described as green or yellow shade.

Heliodor most commonly occurs as an accessory mineral in granites, and is usually found in cavities and in granite pegmatites. Heliodor is mostly found in Brazil, Madagascar, Namibia, Nigeria, Pakistan, Russia, Sri Lanka and Zimbabwe.

Astrologically, Heliodor energies are said to complement the zodiac birth signs of Cancer and Sagittarius. Heliodor energies are alike the energy elements of sun and fire in nature.

Historically, Heliodor was distinguished as a form of Beryl by the Roman historian "Pliny". Heliodor belongs to the family of Beryl gemstones. Therefore, Heliodor is also known as the yellow emerald or golden Beryl. Heliodor has been called the stone of the "Gods", and the gateway to the light. Heliodors name originates from a combination of Greek words, "Helios" and" door", which in fact means, "Gift from the Sun".

Metaphysically, Heliodor is known to bring balance to the Yang/ Male aspects and characteristics of self. Heliodor is considered to work effectively great for both Male and Females energies combined. Heliodor is an amazingly positive crystal, that brings vibrancy and generosity. Metaphysically Heliodor will simulate the Solar Plexus, Third - Eye and Crown chakra energy centres.

Uses and Purposes

Heliodors yellow colouring shades may vary remarkably, so it can be very difficult to distinguish between Heliodor and golden Beryl. Heliodor crystals, in some cases can grow to extremely large. This stone is often associated with Aquamarine also. Heliodor is also recognised for its impeccable golden crystals.

The warmth and glow of the yellow stone has been said to enhance the wearer's intuition, compassion and promote a positive wellbeing. It can help us to break free from the blockages and energy barriers, allowing one to connect and tap into our own inner strengths, thus making us feel completely in control, and responsible for our own lives.

Heliodor will also assist one in developing a deeper sense of maturity. As we grow, we can gain the appropriate knowledge and levels of understanding to support us as we rise into our truest and greatest potential. Therefore, Heliodor will support, and allow

us to feel balanced and prepared for anything
practically. Heliodor can be oiled or heat treated
although the process of heat treatment can often
extinguish the stone's yellow shades resulting in a clear
or even an Aquamarine Blue shade of stone.
Irradiation can reverse this effect.

Pure Beryl is actually colourless, but various impurities
presented within the stone which are then categorise
as different stones, alike Heliodor. Beryl has an
adequate scale of hardness and therefore it's a great
stone to sculpt into jewellery, and other various
ornamental keepsakes.

Mind, Body & Soul Healing Therapies

Emotional Healing Energy - Heliodor brings with it, a sense of compassion, kindness, sympathy, and understanding in one. It can terminate duality and judgement from the one who wears it. It makes it easy for the wearer to confront any difficult and delicate issues.

The vibrational energies of Heliodor can balance the conscious and psychic levels of our human nature. Heliodor is an excellent stone for those who have survived some forms of abuse and traumas in their lives. It makes the wearer become more optimistically positive and take a tactile approach towards one's self and life. Heliodor supports the bearer to accomplish their goals, desires, and dreams.

<u>Physical Healing Energy</u> - Heliodor is said to strengthen the immune system, and is a purifying stone. Heliodor is handy to keep around during the season of infectious colds and flus. Heliodor is said to treat problems and conditions of the liver, spleen, and pancreas. It can aid fatigue and exhaustion.

Heliodor can be used as a calming remedy for healing jaundice, the small intestine, diarrhoea, nausea, constipation, and cramps. Heliodor can be used for treating ailments associated with the eyes such as long-sightedness, short-sightedness, or infection.

Heliodors qualities can directly enhance one's mental power, self-confidence as well as one's physical strength. Additionally, Heliodor is also thought to invoke the bright and sunny rays of knowledge and learning that stimulates the ability of the brain to function more effectively.

<u>Chakra Healing Energy</u> - Heliodors positive and strong energies connect directly to the Solar Plexus chakra centre, boosting one's vitality and energy levels. Heliodor radiates the energy of vitality alike the sun, therefore this stone will help the wearer to raise, transmute and eliminate lower negative energies of stress, worry, fear, and other feelings of similar low vibration that may cause anxieties. Heliodor is often described as the "Sunshine Stone". Its warmth projects, and ultimately protects and enhances our wellbeing's, and is an extremely effective confidence boosting crystal.

<u>Activating, Charging, Cleansing & Purifying methods for your Heliodor.</u> Heliodor can be charged and cleansed by the sun and sage. Although, moon-light and smudging are the safest options for cleansing all your precious crystals and gemstones.

Lemon Quartz

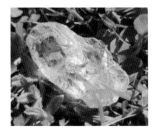 Lemon Quartz presents us with a vibrant citrus zest the deeper the tone the greater the quality. The Quartz part of its name is derived from the Greek word for ice, "Krustallos". Lemon Quartz, also known as "Oro Verde Quartz", is Quartz that has been irradiated to achieve the beautiful gold, green- -lemon colouring. Lemon Quartz gains its distinguishing yellow colouring because of it being an irradiated crystal. This natural radiation treated crystal, is perfectly safe, however because of its irradiated state it does contain high vibration energy levels, and those souls who are sensitive to crystalline vibration energy, may find it to be too overwhelming. Lemon Quartz is a hexagonal silicon dioxide crystal.

Lemon Quartz is mostly found in Africa, Brazil, Canada, France, Madagascar, Russia, Scotland, Spain and in parts of the United States of America.

Astrologically, Lemon Quartz energies are said to complement the zodiac birth signs of Gemini. Lemon Quartz energies are alike the energy element of fire in nature. Lemon Quartz also resonates with the number 9.

Historically, Lemon Quartz is known throughout as a good luck or charm type gemstone, because of the vibrant, zesty, cheery, sunny, and full of life energies that Lemon Quartz radiates. Therefore, Lemon Quartz is particularly handy to keep on one's person when looking for a "bright" and "positive" outcome to any situation.

Metaphysically, Lemon Quartz has a fresh, vibrant nature, and feel of summer. This gemstone works well in female and male jewellery as it adds a fresh energy feeling, and will attract for the wearer a magnificently powerful vibration of anew fresh zesty energies in abundance.

Uses and Purposes

Lemon Quartz can to be used to attract and align one to new opportunities and experiences for abundance. It's used by many to count one's blessings, as lemon Quartz will assist one in manifestation, by lightening one's energy field to a sunnier state of bliss. Lemon Quartz will attract opportunities into one's experiences, so if you are taking your driving test or an exam of some sort, or are applying for a promotion at work. Maybe you are applying for a job, or going for a job interview, then keep a piece of lemon quartz on your person to attract abundance and prosperity. It may also attract to the bearer money during times of hardship or emergencies, hence another reason why it's known as a good luck stone, to attract abundance of whatever nature needed.

Lemon Quartz will also support and boost one's self confidence, as well as self-assurance. Lemon Quartz will amplify energy surrounding our thoughts, and allows you to see clearly and receive information intuitively. This aids in clarity of thought, strengthens communication, and emotional balance. Therefore,

Lemon Quartz will enable the wearer to think more effectively and quickly, when making direct decisions. The zesty energy of Lemon Quartz also allows the bearer / healer of the gemstone energies to create a peaceful and positive state of balance within one's aura, mind, and body combined.

Although, Citrine and Lemon Quartz are fairly similar gemstones, the difference between Citrine and Lemon Quartz is in the saturation and tone of their colour. Gemstone dealers don't separate the two, and refer to Citrine alike yellow Quartz. Lemon Quartz truly dazzles its vibrancy when set into white or yellow Gold and Silver.

Mind, Body & Soul Healing Therapies

Emotional Healing Energy - Lemon Quartz
felicitates and aids one with a sense from within of
higher, sharper and a clearer thinking ability to become
bounteous in creativity. Lemon Quartz has qualities
that remind the wearer / carrier of what is ultimately
important, and for us to remain in continual gratitude
for all things. Lemon Quartz will also bring the wearer
a sense of optimism, contentment, and warm energies
alike the sun, while it enhances positivity and peaceful
energies to those wearing the crystal, and to their
surrounding environment. Lemon Quartz can free the
wearer of any built-up anxiety, as its energy has the
ability to reduce stress and tensions.

Physical Healing Energy - Lemon Quartz speeds up
the recovery process after illness and surgery, as it
increases your metabolic rate. Lemon Quartz can also
be used as an excellent crystal for dieters, as it can
assist to reduce one's food cravings and can also
reduce nicotine cravings if you desire to give up

smoking. Lemon Quartz will assist the wearer to focus the mind on one's dreams and desires, therefore allowing one to set physical targets and goals to work towards.

Chakra Healing Energy - Lemon Quartz radiates healing properties and vitality energy alike the sunshine, so that it can ultimately attract to the wearer energies of clarity, peace, joy, happiness, and harmony as the crystal has the power to balance the energy in the solar plexus chakra centre. Lemon Quartz is a powerful crystal that heralds' energies that will allow one to access and attain deeper levels of energy states within meditation, so one can explore the realms found within these inner dimensions. Lemon Quartz is an extraordinary crystal for healers when scrying. It will support and create a clearer channel within "mediation", between your angels and spirit guides alike. Therefore, Lemon Quartz strengthens the connection and bond with higher self, creator, and loved ones who have crossed over and also with souls who are present, whilst having a positive and balancing effect on our emotional wellbeing, bringing balance and harmony to one's mind, body, and soul.

<u>Activating, Charging, Cleansing & Purifying methods for your Lemon Quartz.</u> Lemon Quartz can be charged and cleansed by reiki and white sage. Although, moon-light and smudging are the safest options for cleansing all your precious crystals and gemstones.

Merlinite

 Merlinite is considered to be a stone of duality, as is exhibited by its mystical black and white appearance. Merlinite consists of a variety of Opal, and often has an opalescent sheen. Merlinite is black and white, although its ranges in colour from grey to black. The black can be Romanechite or Psilomelane, or it may be black Dendritic inclusions within the stone. The white within the stone can be a blend of white Chalcedony or white Quartz, depending on the individual stone.

Merlinite is also known as Dendritic Opal. Dendric Opal is a form of Opal that has dark tubular or orbicular patterns composed of manganese, and often appear as markings / shapes alike ferns or trees.

Merlinite has been located on a remote island in the Indian ocean and consists of a unique blend of quartz, feldspar, and other minerals. Merlinite has also been found in a mine in New Mexico.

Astrologically, Merlinite energies are said to complement the zodiac birth signs of Gemini and Pisces. Merlinite energies are alike the energy elements of water in nature.

Historically, Merlinite, the name gifted to this particular stone, gives a clear indication to the spiritual powers and qualities this stone encompasses. "Mystic Merlinite" is the common name given to this extremely magical and powerful stone.

Metaphysically, Merlinite is an attractive stone in appearance, with white and black both blending and balancing into each other, beautifully becoming one. Therefore, this particular stone reflects the dark & light within one's self, and combined it also represents the classical symbol of Yin & Yang, and showing us that dark and light are separate aspects of the same whole. Merlinite is also a crystal highly regarded for its balancing and blending energies, which encourages equilibrium.

Uses and Purposes

Merlinite is a stone considered to grant us access into the Akashic records. Merlinite heralds the secrets to all magic from shamans, magicians and light workers united, and the spirit realms. Mystic Merlinite will support and aid a deeper connection and communication between the user, allowing one to experience clearer psychic visions, and channel energies to and from our etheric teachers, ancestors, and guides from higher spiritual realms.

The wearer needs to be mindful and aware that while Merlinite may produce many magical benefits, it can easily provide the reverse effect and put you in contact with the darker levels of yourself, that you have buried deeply within in your subconscious self. Merlinite is also said to attract powerful magic and good luck energies into the existence of any warrior who dares wear or carry it as a crystal companion on their journey. Therefore, Merlinite is renowned for its mystical and magical energies that one can access while journeying either in the physical or meditative sense.

Many that use Merlinite, including myself, have had experiences of being within the presence of alchemists and wizards from the past in present within vision, signs and memories seen and felt within meditations, and during healing or testing times. People have additionally mentioned that the realizations they had come too about themselves and life as a whole when using this stone, have led to a many magnificent transformations of self, and these insights brought positive life changes. Merlinite ultimately promotes self-love, self-belief, self-forgiveness, self-knowledge, self-control, self-awareness, and self-power. Merlinite will support the wearer to balance energies within both light and dark.

Mind, Body & Soul Healing Therapies

Emotional Healing Energy – Merlinite crystal contains mystical energies that can aid one to acknowledge and release deeply held emotional patterns and wounds from the past. Merlinite used in regression meditation, will bring visions and wisdom, so that one can gain a greater knowledge of self and one's inner wisdom, bringing in healing, harmony and peace, to this present lifetime. Merlinite can additionally gift the wearer to recognise one's natural talents and gifts, so that you may use your gifts to the fullest for the greater good of yourself and all. Merlinite guides its users to become progressively aware and self-awakened, as this magical stone will assist the wearer to become more aligned and mindful in time.

Physical Healing Energy - Merlinite gemstone aids the wearer in healing of the heart. Its mystic powers are capable in aiding one with improvement and development of blood flow circulation. Merlinite can support treatments and healing of the veins and arteries. Merlinite will also give relief to the wearer, if one suffers from headaches or migraine. Merlinite will generate and support ones overall well- being. Merlinite is a positive stone that will attract balance to the body, and assist one with great growth.

<u>Chakra Healing Energy</u> - Merlinite attracts to one's Solar Plexus chakra its most protective, positive, and powerful energies. Therefore, this crystal is favoured and common among healers to enhance and encompass the will and magical power within ones Solar Plexus. Merlinite conceals energies that will align and un-block negative energy blockages between the 3rd and 6th chakras. Merlinite will activate one's Third Eye chakra allowing the bearer of this gemstone to remove the veil of illusion, giving one a deeper connection to one's intuition along with a clearer sense of balance. Merlinite ultimately brings harmony within the energy centres, between the Solar Plexus chakra and the Third Eye chakra.

<u>Activating, Charging, Cleansing & Purifying methods for your Merlinite.</u> Merlinite can be charged and cleansed by reiki and sage. Moon-light and smudging are the safest options for cleansing all your precious crystals and gemstones.

Pyrite

 Pyrite is notoriously known as "Fool's Gold," and is also referred to as Iron Pyrite, and in Germany, "Cat's Gold." Granted Pyrite is commonly nicknamed "Fool's Gold," there is nothing foolish about this glittering mineral. Pyrite has dazzled many, and many have mistaken this mineral as real gold.

Pyrite is lighter in colour than Gold, deceptive to the touch it seems harder, but is more brittle than Gold. It can't be scratched or marked easily.

Hidden within its gleaming beauty it's a stone of rich fire, a rock that can be sparked back to life by striking it against stone or metal.

Pyrite gems have been located in many various destinations worldwide, from Britain, Chile, Italy, North America, Peru and Spain.

Astrologically, Pyrite energies are said to complement the zodiac birth signs of Leo. Although Pyrites energies encompasses the elements in nature of the earth, it also resonates with fire energy, thus symbolizes the warmth of the sun. "Pyr" is the Greek word for fire.

Historically, Pyrite was also used in the past by dishonest mine owners, to salt the mines convincing naïve bodies they were still actively producing gold.

Metaphysically, Pyrite is a unique protector, as it draws energy from the Earth through the physical body and into one's aura, creating a defensive shield against emotional attacks, physical harm, environmental pollutants, and all means of negative energies. Pyrite contains the energies and ability to attract and generate wealth, by the correct use of one's own personal Solar Plexus power.

Uses and Purposes

Pyrite not only stimulates the Third chakra, it also has a positive effect on the Second chakra energy centre, as it enhancing will power and highly stimulates the ability to see behind the masquerade to what is real. Thus, allowing the wearer to project their personal will, and tap into one's owns abilities and personal potential when using or needing to protect nature and our planet. In other cases, one might have to stand up for important issues to defend themselves or others.

Many Healers use Pyrite as a Talisman, to support the user with building inner confidence and boldness of one's spirit. As well as these qualities, Pyrite attracts an abundance of greater will, too assist one with committing assertiveness to projects or promises, so these can be carried through to completion. Pyrite stimulates the creative flow, ideas and actions of the wearer. Pyrite is a powerful, protective, shielding stone and is excellent to wear or carry as astral armour, to deflect danger, negative energies that could potentially harm.

A piece of Pyrite in the home, workplace or altar, can energizes the area around it and can instantaneously increase one's vitality, giving an energy boost alike the sun. It is especially helpful when one is travelling away from home, or undertaking heavy or hazardous work tasks.

Mind, Body & Soul Healing Therapies

Emotional Healing Energy - Pyrite can also guard against manipulation, control, and criticism from others, allowing one to harness the powers to resist, without becoming angry, emotional, upset, and attached. Encouraging the individual to overcome any fears and take action against the manipulator.
Pyrite is composed of positive energy, and is extremely helpful in bringing one out of their comfort zone, as confidence grows within its wearer.

Pyrite can assist one with mindfulness, and the transmutation of lower energies and any heavyhearted thoughts fixated on un-necessary unpleasantness and discomfort. Therefore, Pyrite can also reveal and relieve us of anxiety and frustration, as it reflects back to self.

Pyrite also allows one to see beyond the surface to what lies truly behind the words and actions of others. Whereas Pyrite is masculine in nature, it's a stone of action. It brings vitality to the bearer. Pyrite will enhance the protective and assertive male energies in both men and women. For men, it increases or instils feelings of confidence in one's masculinity and supports the expression of male eroticism. For women, it can increase or instil feelings also of confidence, and overall boost one's feelings of self- worth.

<u>Physical Healing Energy</u> - Pyrite is known to overcome physical and intellectual fatigue due to over-working, over -thinking and tiredness of the central and peripheral nervous system. It increases vitality, and stimulating blood flow to the brain. This then increase one's mental clarity, memory and allows one a superior focus. Pyrite mineral shields the body from contagious diseases as well as environmental pollutants.
Pyrite has also been used in treatments to fight a wide range of highly infectious diseases, and viruses. It can

be extremely beneficial in cases where no resolution seems possible. Pyrite brings a ray of light and hope just alike the sun. It can also protect and fight against common colds, flu, fungal infections and skin diseases.

Pyrite supports the wearer to paint a picture of perfect health and well-being, drawing on powerful universal healing energies, which can also balance energies between the mind and body, and have a positive effect on any negative energies or imbalances that can occur within psychosomatic disease.

Chakra Healing Energy - Pyrite can connect the energies from the Solar Plexus chakra, down to the root chakra, and ground them onto the earths plane for manifestations. Pyrite protects the solar plexus energy of the wearer against negative external energy forces trying to penetrate the energetic aura field. Pyrite is associated with fire, creativity, and passion. Pyrite attracts a protective golden vibration of positive energy to the solar plexus.

Pyrite inspires creativity in art and the sciences, as well as many other developments curiously, in those that can recognize the fundamental perfection and harmonious beauty of the energetic flow within nature and our entire universe. Pyrite's energy is extremely empowering and elevating to one's spirit.

Pyrite used also within spirituality teachings, healings and rituals as this mineral brings balance and order. It restores the forever changing balance of power in the user's favour.

Pyrite is a wonder worker. It will assist one when it comes to dealing with getting to the root of karmic debt. Allowing all energies to un-spiral related to karmic, patterns, cycles, inner shadow work, and cosmic ties, to be transmuted and healed.

<u>Activating, Charging, Cleansing & Purifying methods for your Pyrite.</u> Avoid water and intense sunlight when cleansing Pyrite. Moon-light and smudging are the safest options for cleansing all your precious crystals and gemstones.

Rutilated Quartz

 Rutilated Quartz is a type of Quartz with a rutile needle effect embedded within the quartz. The rutile needles can be golden, silvery, or reddish, which is what "rutile" means in Latin, or they may even have a green hint within on very rare occasion.

Rutilated Quartz hardness measures at 7 on Mohs scale. Quartz 6/ 6.5 is Rutile. Rutilated Quartz is created when Rutile forms within a Quartz stone.

Rutilated Quartz gems have been located in many various destinations worldwide, from Australia, Brazil, France, Italy, Madagascar, Sweden and within eastern parts of the United States of America.

Astrologically, Rutilated Quartz energies are said to complement the zodiac birth signs of Gemini and Taurus. Rutilated Quartz energies encompasses the elements of air and fire in nature.

Historically, Rutilated Quartz, through-out time has been regarded to be a highly energizing stone, and is said to be particularly effective for getting things moving energetically. Rutilated Quartz was used by our ancient ancestors to channel energies and its motion through-out our body's systems. They used Rutilated Quartz energies to bring harmony and balance back within the chakras, as well as un-block energy, returning and resetting your energy to its natural and normal flow.

Metaphysically, Rutilated Quartz is also used metaphysically to deflect negative energies such as, psychic attacks, unwanted energetic leeches and magical interferences. Some intuitive sources say that Rutilated Quartz crystal will assist with mental focus and concentration.

Uses and Purposes

Rutilated Quartz is said to be a powerful stone, and its energies can attract love, stable souls, and more attractive and loyal relationships into one's life. Rutilated Quartz is said to also be able to ease loneliness and relieve one from any guilt, bringing the carrier of this precious gemstone an abundance of happiness.

The energy that lies within the golden rutile stone is known to hold an extraordinary energy, that will support the wearer to cope most efficiently in difficult situations. With the added extra energy boost of Rutilated Quartz it can also enhance one's energy of personal will power. Carrying a golden Rutilated Quartz crystal will most certainly make life easier for the wearer of this stone. This stone can be indeed very powerful, and may move your life in a new direction rapidly.

Mind, Body & Soul Healing Therapies

Emotional Healing Energy - Rutilated Quartz is said to be very helpful in identifying the causes of mental issues and attachments. Rutilated Quartz is used also metaphysically to help one to shift stagnant energies, so one can fully function in a forward motion and flow within their life. Rutilated Quartz will bring a harmonious, stabilizing balance emotionally to ones thought patterns, by gently supporting the processes. This will allow the wearer to emotionally and mentally become mindful of their actions and reactions to all situations with clarity. The stone will draw off negative energy and can break down the barriers to spiritual progress, letting go of the past, allowing one to move forward freely. As Rutilated Quartz is known to assist the wearer in diminishing any fears.

Rutilated Quartz is also said to increase one's self-reliance and confidence, giving the wearer the ability to find one's own way within their life's journey.

<u>Physical Healing Energy</u> ~ Rutilated Quartz is a healing crystal, that will open the aura field to allow healing. Therefore, Rutilated Quartz will enhance energies and allow a freer flow, so that one can to attain deeper levels of forgiveness within our healings.

This particular healing crystal at a physical level, absorbs mercury poisoning from the blood, nerves, muscles, and the intestinal tract. Rutilated Quartz also can assist in treating chronic conditions within the respiratory system, such as and bronchitis.

Rutilated Quartz stimulates growth and regeneration of one's cells and can be used to balance the thyroid, as well as aid repairs to torn tissues. Rutilated Quartz can also be used to assist with treating conditions within infertility. It is also said to encourage the repellent of parasites.

Rutilated Quartz is also widely known to be beneficial for supporting souls with food disorders. Rutilated Quartz is also a magic mystical crystal, often used as a "diagnostic tool" which can help discover the true cause of an ailment, and is also known to be an excellent stone at assisting with the decision-making processes.

This gemstone has a vitality that is excellent for energy depletion, exhaustion or chronic fatigue it will rejuvenate and recharge one's aura.

Chakra Healing Energy - Rutilated Quartz spiritually, is said to have the perfect balance of captured cosmic light and is an illuminator for the soul, to light the way ahead in life. Rutilated Quartz will assist you to receive spiritual knowledge and guidance, to help you to gain concentration and mental clarity, as well as promoting spiritual growth. Rutilated Quartz will stimulate and boost the solar plexus energy centre if carry it on your person.

Rutilated Quartz also transmutes and assists one to transform negative energy into positive energies, allowing one to cleanses and energizes their aura field.

Rutilated Quartz energizes the higher mind and can activate energies from the heart chakra, up to the crown chakra, allowing a greater connection between the psychic and spiritual realms. Rutilated Quartz is often used within spiritual communications, meditation, dream work, and is often used to heighten and develop psychic gifts. Rutilated Quartz will enhance one's telepathic abilities and can be used to assist with astral travel, scrying and channelling. This is a magnificent and powerful stone that can shift stagnant energies within meridians and areas where the physical energy is lethargic.

Activating, Charging, Cleansing & Purifying methods for your Rutilated Quartz. Rutilated Quartz can be charged and cleansed by reiki, sage or water. Moonlight and smudging are the safest options for cleansing all your precious crystals and gemstones.

Sunshine Aura Quartz

 Sunshine Aura Quartz is the name given to this adjoining crystal in the broader group of crystals referred to as 'Aura Quartz'. This particular crystal is known as Sunshine Aura Quartz.

Sunshine Aura Quartz attracts and encourages the Sun on the carrier, by bringing a high vibrational energy to one energy fields. This then allows for an enhanced energetic healing energy to enter into the aura.

Sunshine Aura Quartz gems can be located in many various crystal and precious gemstone out-lets worldwide.

Astrologically, Sunshine Aura Quartz energies are said to complement the zodiac birth signs of Aquarius, although Sunshine Aura is considered an overall astrological stone for all zodiac signs. Sunshine Aura encompasses elements in nature alike the earth and fire.

Historically, Sunshine Aura Quartz is created when Clear Quartz goes under a special process, through which the surface of the Quartz has been bonded with vaporised platinum, gold, and other trace metals. This then results in the crystals characteristic becoming altered to a pale yellow/orange colour, with a beautiful iridescent rainbow effect that "glitters" and radiates alike the Sun

Metaphysically, Sunshine Aura Quartz frequencies have a powerful connection to the solar plexus chakra, as well as the energies strong enough to connect to all physical chakras, opening and stimulating these chakras, so that one has a positive attitude towards all of life's experiences.

Uses and Purposes

Sunshine Aura Quartz is an inspiring crystal and will connect us with our power within of creativity. It encourages us to bring these expressions, ideas and arts out into the world. It's attuned to the loving energies of the Universe, this crystal will aid one to see and connect to the beauty that surrounds us all, with the high energy contained within

Sunshine Aura Quartz encourages a new-found enthusiasm for life, and one will feel overwhelmed with joy, laughter, and happiness, allowing one's inner child to come to light from within. Sunshine aura Quartz is known to bring about the most positive energies of light and love brightly shining, allowing one to see the innocent side of any situation.
Sunshine Aura Quartz brings additional light into naturally dark or dingy spaces. Therefore, Sunshine aura quartz is really supportive to those living in areas where the winters are long and days are dark for longer periods of times. Carry Sunshine Aura Quartz to combat seasonal depression or tiredness, as Sunshine

Aura supports souls affected by the darker seasons and to aid absorption of vitamins A, D and E

Sunshine Aura Quartz placed in the centre of a crystal grid, sacred space, social gathering or workspace, will bring an abundance of enthusiastic energies of light, love, laughter.

Mind, Body & Soul Healing Therapies

Emotional Healing Energy – Sunshine Aura Quartz crystals provide one's emotional body with a calm and relaxing energy and gives a highly soothing and healing sense to one's aura. These crystals are uplifting to one's spirit, as they promote exceptional energies to enter into one's aura field, that aid the wearer to release any negative energies, doubts and past wounds. Sunshine Aura Quartz encourages us to look at how we take responsibility for our own happiness and success, other than looking to place this responsibility onto others, allowing us the freedoms to overcome the feelings of disappointments that have been with in life, as well as allowing us space to heal old traumas, bitterness and hurt. Sunshine Aura promotes personal powers of, good self-esteem, self-confidence, trust in ourselves and others.

Sunshine Aura Quartz can help the carrier to raise one's own vibrational energy, so that a harmonious and peaceful view of the world can be attained, while one harnesses and is able to radiate these qualities whatever situation one finds oneself to be in. Sunshine Aura Quartz is known to aid and allow the wearer the ability to see the lessons that can be learnt, whatever the outcome of those particular experiences or situations one found oneself in.

Physical Healing Energy – Sunshine Aura Quartz energies are enhanced by the coating of precious metals onto these crystals, therefore they become master-healers and high-vibrational stones that can be used to aid aliments and other various health conditions. Sunshine Aura Quartz is an extremely powerful energy amplifier for absorbing, healing, releasing, regulating, and storing energies within the body.

79

Sunshine Aura Quartz carries a high level of life force energies that will assist one with cleansing and enhancing the efficiency of one's organs, stimulating the energy and immune systems, by bringing the body back into alignment, harmony and balance. It's considered powerfully positive for removing toxins from the body. It will also assist in relieving constipation and aiding with digestive issues. These crystals are considered especially beneficial for oxygenating the blood, as well as cleansing and stimulating the thymus, thyroid and pineal glands. Sunshine aura Quartz is also used for treatments of the gall bladder, liver, the nervous system, pancreas and spleen.

Chakra Healing Energy - Sunshine Aura Quartz has a strong energetic connection to the Solar Plexus, therefore can assist one to activate and balance the energies within the solar plexus. At a spiritual level, it is expansive and protective, inspiring optimism within the carrier. Sunshine Aura brings the wearer of this crystal into spiritual alignment and can harmonize the energies between all of the chakra energy centres. Sunshine Aura is said to activate and cleanse one's Solar Plexus, to release the bearer of the crystal from traumatic negative energy blocks from past painful experiences.

Sunshine Aura Quartz will infuse the whole system with health, vitality, and energies of that alike our Sun, if placed in the centre of any healing crystal layout. It's a stone of joy, happiness, light and love for life.

Activating, Charging, Cleansing & Purifying methods for your Sunshine Aura Quartz. Sunshine Aura Quartz_ can be charged and cleansed by the sun and sage. Although, moon-light and smudging are the safest options for cleansing all your precious crystals and gemstones.

Tigers Eye

 Tigers Eye is considered and Widley celebrated as an ancient talisman, its magical, mysterious, powerful and protective energies are said to be feared by some. Tigers Eye is known as the "all-seeing, all-knowing eye," its seen to grant the wearer the ability to observe everything, even from afar. Tigers Eye, also referred to as "Tiger Iron", simply because the colour within Tiger's Eye is mainly made by Iron oxide deposits within this gemstone. Tiger's Eye is primarily comprised of silicon dioxide. Tigers Eye can vary in colours from brown, blue, green, golden- yellow, or red. An extremely similar stone to Tigers Eye is Hawks Eye, this gemstone comes in shades of blues and grey.

Tigers Eye gemstones have been located in many various destinations worldwide, from Africa, Australia, China, Namibia, Prieska, and within some areas in the United States of America.

Astrologically, Tigers Eye energies are said to complement the zodiac birth signs of Gemini. Tigers Eye energies encompasses the element of earth and the planet Mercury in nature.

Historically, Tiger's Eye in ancient Egypt, was understood to have provided the wearer with the protection of Ra, the Egyptian "Sun God". It's also known that the ancient Egyptians would attach Tigers eye to wigs and mounted them onto the eyes in their deity statues to express divine vision. It's said that they would also use this particular stone to felicitate meditations and astral travel. Tiger's Eye would also be carried in battle by the soldiers of the Roman Empire, they would use Tigers Eye to aid one's energies with the gifts of bravery and foresight in battle, as well as use them to deflect weapons.

Metaphysically, Tigers Eye is a highly regarded gemstone throughout history as a stone of protection for one's self and one's properties, by reflecting negative energies of malevolence, or threats from the external environment.

Uses and Purposes

Tiger's Eye can be used as a support stone. It will gift the wearer the strength and determination to overcome fears during competitions, exams, performances, public events, and all manors of tests. Tigers Eye counsels one against complacency, and encourages one to step out of their "Comfort Zone" in-order to grow and experiment with one's artistic and creative abilities and talents.

Many people carry Tigers Eye as a stone of luck and good fortune. It attracts a steady flow of wealth to the wearer. Tiger's Eye is an ideal gemstone for any souls setting out in business for the first time, or wishing to make unsettling or challenging career changes in the near future. Tigers Eye supports necessary change in all aspects of one's life, while gifting a better understanding of the causes and effects that change brings to each situation.

Mind, Body & Soul Healing Therapies

Physical Healing Energy – Tigers Eye placed on either side of the head, will encompass all energies and re-balance the "Control Centre", the brains hemispheres. Tigers Eye also placed on one's reproductive organs, may stimulate fertility and heighten one's sexual experiences. Tiger's Eye is acknowledged and used to heal disorders of the eyes, and it is also known to aid and enhance night vision. Tigers Eye can aid one's respiratory system to calm, relax, and relieve asthma attacks. Tigers Eye is additionally known to aid with throat issues

Tiger's Eye conventionally is used to align and strengthen the spine, as well as stimulate the repair of broken bones. Tiger's Eye can additionally ease problems with the stomach and gall bladder. Though traditionally Tiger's Eye is thought to be a blood booster and bodyguard. It can aid against angina and help lower blood pressure, while increasing vitality and vigour, and restoring balance back into the body on every level. It's also is believed to boost the endocrine system, bringing one's bio-chemical rhythms back into balance.

Emotional Healing Energy – Tigers Eye is used to boost one's emotional stability. Its renowned to reduces anxiety caused by feelings of isolation, incompetence, and all emotional insecurities. Tiger's Eye is exceptional for healing internal issues of self-criticism, confidence and worth, assisting to unblock one's creativity, so one may herald a sense of freedom from fear. Tigers Eye is extremely favourable crystal for settling internal conflicts, especially those initiated by anger, ego, fear, jealousy or pride.

Tigers Eye is a beneficial aid and ally for the emotional side of oneself, as it brings balances back into one's mind, all emotional energies and thoughts attached. Thus, allowing any scattered thoughts that separate us emotional, along with feelings and information to become transformed together in such a way, that it starts to makes sense.

Tigers Eye brings focus and stability, enabling one to make greater decisions from a detached space of will and wisdom, not present emotionally attached place.

Chakra Healing Energy – Tigers Eye grounds the beaming energy of the Sun rays onto Earths plane, stimulating ones Root, Sacral and Solar Plexus Chakras. Golden Tigers Eye brings with it an abundance of energies to support and boost one's spirituality, vitality and will power. Tigers Eye is an ever-observant crystal, which will gift one with a connection and sensational sharpness, that in turn will heighten one's senses and psychic inner visions.

Tiger's Eye is most certainly a stone for those set collectively gathering knowledge and wisdom. It encourages one to use their personal Solar Plexus energy powers most perfectly and wisely. Therefore, if one can harness Tiger's Eye energies for the betterment of all, the crystal will work with you to strengthening the will and integrity of the intention set, in order for it to be to manifest in at the highest level.

Tigers Eye teaches one integrity, bringing the bearer of this stone an awareness of one's own needs, rather than wants, as well as gifting one with a greater understanding of the need's others hold too.

<u>Activating, Charging, Cleansing & Purifying methods</u>
<u>for your Tigers Eye.</u> Tigers can be charged and
cleansed by sage, earth burial, bury in sea salt and
water. Although, moon-light and smudging are the
safest options for cleansing all your precious crystals
and gemstones.

Yellow Apatite

Yellow Apatite is known for its positive use of personal power to achieve goals. Yellow Apatite can comprise from yellow to green, or a deep golden yellow alike the Sun. The name Apatite is acknowledged as a Greek word, meaning "to deceive". This is down to the variation of colours and compilation in which this stone is presented, making it simple to mistake for other minerals. It may be sourced in yellow, green, grey, brown or blue, and on some occasions colourless.

.

Yellow Apatite gems have been located in many various destinations worldwide, from Canada, Brazil, Burma, India, Kenya, Madagascar, Mexico. Norway, South Africa, Sri Lanka and areas within the United States of America.

Astrologically, Yellow Apatite energies are said to complement the zodiac birth signs of Gemini. Yellow Apatite encompasses an element in nature alike fire.

Historically, Yellow Apatite is also referred to as Gold, or Golden Apatite. It's one of the purest crystals, with a vibration of strength, inner will, mental clarity, and magical energy towards manifestations, that help one with manifesting their dreams and desires.

Metaphysically, Yellow Apatite it's a dual action stone. It can give one the ability to clear away negativity and confusion, stimulating the intellect, to expand wisdom, knowledge and truth which can be used for personal spiritual growth, or for the collective good of all.

Uses and Purposes

Yellow Apatite is a stone associated with animal conservation. This particular crystal is composed of the mineral phosphate that is made up from the bones, teeth, tusks, horns and antlers of all vertebrate animals.

Yellow Apatite is particularly useful to have around when one is starting new ventures. This crystal will bring positive energies to support and enhance creative ideas, assisting the bearer to manifest these ideas into reality. Yellow Apatite will assist one with developing the required business skills needed, to create a comfortable way living from one's passions and gifts.

Yellow Apatite is a crystal that assists one with promoting healing, promoting one to have a humanitarian outlook on life, allowing one to become of greater service to others.

Yellow Apatite comes with a caution for those with a surplus of natural confidence. This particular crystal may make one with similar natures, become a little too self-assured. This may be seen as irrigatable to others.

Yellow Apatite can prevent tiredness and boredom, and can provide one with an invigorating vitality. It can assist one to become more self-confident, outgoing and optimistic. Therefore, it helps one become livelier and increases one's drive, bringing positive energies that will motivate one into getting things done.

Yellow Apatite can boost one's aura with positive energy, providing the carrier with the courage to take risks, gifting one the clarity to know which risks are worth taking and which ones are not.

Yellow Apatite is a stone known to support the wearer with enlarging one's capability to process and retain new information.

Mind, Body & Soul Healing Therapies

Emotional Healing Energy - Yellow Apatite is a positive crystal that brings with it rays of hope, joy, vitality, and a sunny optimism outlook. It harnesses the power to heal past negative patterns, providing one with the energy to manifest creative thoughts and actions needed to achieve one's goals in present. Yellow Apatite helps one with releasing old blockages that may limit one's acceptance or perception of prosperity or abundance. It will assist one to overcome any fear of success. Yellow Apatite can assist women, not just men, by allowing the energies of Apatite in to support and strengthen the male energies of their personality, developing courage, self-esteem and confidence to be able to step out of your comfort zone and into one's personal power with determination, purpose and pride.

Physical Healing Energy - Yellow Apatite will assist one to balances the appetite. It is a supportive crystal of healthy eating and the digestive system. It can be an aid in weight loss or enhancing the energetic effects of exercise. Yellow Apatite helps heal bones and teeth, and will assist one with repairs of joint issues and cartilage pain, as well as help one to improve posture. Yellow Apatite stimulates the metabolism and the endocrine system and is used to assist with elimination of toxins in the body.

Chakra Healing Energy - Yellow Apatite will stimulate, activate and stabilizes energies within the solar plexus chakra centre, allowing one to release stagnant negative energy blockages within this particular centre. Thus, giving the wearer freedom from negative energies, allowing one to manifest their chosen desires and dreams, that match the frequency of unconditional love and light, for the highest good of all life. This particular solar stone can infuse one's aura with it a sunny, spiritual energy. It will inspire within the wearer an abundance of joy, hope and passion for life, instilling a sense of self-confidence and self-worth. Although Apatite stones used for metaphysical purposes are primarily higher-quality pieces of crystal in blue, green or gold.

Additionally, Yellow apatite helps to enhances and supports development of psychic gifts and is a solar stone of the future, bringing knowledge to those attuned into its frequency.

<u>Activating, Charging, Cleansing & Purifying methods for your Yellow Apatite.</u> Yellow Apatite can be charged and cleansed by earth burial and sun. Although, moon-light and smudging are the safest options for cleansing all your precious crystals and gemstones.

Yellow Calcite

 Calcite is a common stone that can be sourced easily as the calcium carbonate mineral. Calcite is one of the most widely distributed minerals worldwide. It's the cardinal component in limestone, marbles, as well as stalagmites and stalactites. Calcite represents the stable form of calcium carbonate.

Calcite is most probably found as large, colourless, transparent, complex crystals, or prismatic crystals intertwined with other minerals. Calcite can also occur and form as a vein mineral in deposits from hot springs. This can appear in underground caverns as stalactites and stalagmites. Aragonite will polymorph then into Calcite at 470°C.

Calcites compounds range from the shells of marine organisms, such as bivalves and plankton, as well as sedimentary rocks, limestone, metamorphic marble.

Calcite is known to have a unique quality of optical double refraction. This means that if one were to draw a line on a piece of paper, then place a piece of Calcite over the line, when looking through the stone, the line will appear to have then doubled. Therefore, this asset is why Calcite is often used when manifesting intentions/spells to "double the power" of the intention/spell. It is commonly placed on altars, or worn during magical rituals for this purpose. It is an excellent stone when studying the arts and sciences.

Yellow Calcite gemstones have been located in many various destinations worldwide, from Brazil, Czech Republic and Peru.

<u>Astrologically</u>, Yellow Calcite energies are said to complement the zodiac birth signs of Pisces. Yellow Calcite encompasses an element in nature and energy alike water and the planet Neptune.

<u>Historically</u>, Yellow Calcite is considered a Holy stone for the land of their fathers, as Native

Americans consider this particular stone as a great gift bestowed upon them by the Gods.

Metaphysically, Yellow Calcite is a magnificent gemstone, emitting balancing and healing energies used to assist people with hormonal imbalances. It's also commonly used to heal past abuse, hurt and traumas.

Uses and Purposes

Yellow Calcite is known to attract an abundance of positive blessings and prosperity. Therefore, Yellow Calcite is a stone used by many as an attraction charm, to enhance positive energies that one can use to draw in generosity and good luck

Calcite brings energy alike the sun, encouraging one to project out into the world, their most positive gifts, to use these arts and abilities to their fullest advantage and greatest potential to benefit all. Calcite is a stone that brings with its energies of clarity, allowing greater focus within one's thoughts and will bring a strong sense of peace that can settle one's mind. Calcite will encourage one to be more mindful and in the present.

Mind, Body & Soul Healing Therapies

Emotional Healing Energy - Yellow Calcite is an extremely powerful cleanser and amplifier of energy. Calcite is a calming crystal and will support the carrier with energies that can also soothe one's emotions, bringing clarity and a sense of peace, enjoyment and contentment to one's mind. Calcite connects the emotions with the intellect, and is known to stimulate the intellect, helping one organize intellectual thoughts and information as well as boot one's overall energy levels. Therefore, Calcite can return and restore a deeper sense of harmony and balance between the mind, body and soul. Calcite calms the mind, ultimately teaching one greater levels of awareness and understanding.

Yellow Calcite will stimulate greater insights and can aid the carrier with energy that will boost one's memory. It also supports one through difficulties or challenges related with personal or environmental changes in general.

Physical Healing Energy - Yellow Calcite in general, will amplify and increase one's energy levels, allowing one to physically feel freer from tiredness. Calcite will boost one's inner feeling of vitality. Calcite is known to dissolve calcification of the bones. It can restore and help to balances the absorption of calcium within the body, as well as strengthening the joints having positive benefits to one's skeletal system. Calcite is known to cleanse and enhance the functions of the kidneys, pancreas, and spleen. Calcite can assist one to relieve and lessen skin and intestinal conditions, as well as stimulates tissue healing.

Chakra Healing Energy - Yellow Calcite will cleanse and activate the solar plexus chakra energy centre. It is a purifying, protecting, grounding and aligning stone, that will support the carrier to attract energies of inner peace, joy, harmony, unconditional love and oneness. Calcite will ultimately attract positive energies towards the wearer's aura field, bringing one into divine alignment, and when the courier of Calcite crystal is in absolute alignment with "oneness", or collective consciousness, it is said to

100

bring the bearer a multitude of magnificent possibilities. Calcite is considered a spiritual stone, that facilitates the connection or channel for higher consciousness, and to access and develop one's psychic gifts and astral projection. It helps one's mind and body to identify and remember one's souls' experiences, past and present.

Calcite can be used as mirror to reflect what is hidden within oneself, allowing it to come to the surface. Calcite enhances energies so that exploration can be taken. It can be used to assist and support healing within regression meditation. Calcite will aid one's healing within all dimensions of one's past and present, so that one can the flow freely and easily into a prosperous future.

Calcite brings a boost, as does the sun to one's Solar Plexus, and this boost of energetic energies will naturally increase one's personal power and sense of self-worth, esteem and confidence. Calcite is a stone that will gently amplify but simplify, and balance energy within one's self and their environment.

Calcite calls forth a lustrous energy, which encompasses within a spectrum of energy to unblock and activate all the chakras. Therefore, this stone is magical and magnificent and can be used for many a multipurpose, to creates miracles along with a deeper a connection to its scryer and to its source.

<u>Activating, Charging, Cleansing & Purifying methods for your Yellow Calcite.</u> Yellow Calcite can be charged and cleansed by earth, sun and water. Moon-light and smudging are the safest options for cleansing all your precious crystals and gemstones.

Yellow Danburite

Yellow Danburites combinations activate the intellect and higher consciousness from a heart-based perspective. Yellow Danburite is a fairly common mineral, although it's not a signifyingly sought after gemstone. Its appurtenance is silky smooth and shining alike the sun, full of warm radiant energy.

Danburite is a transparent gemstone, comprised from calcium boron silicate and can vary in colours from brown, pink, white, and yellow.

Yellow Danburite gems have been located in many various locations worldwide, from Bolivia, Burma, Japan, Madagascar, Mexico and Russia. The mineral was first discovered in 1839 in Danbury Connecticut, United States of America. Although no gemstone has actually ever came from there.

Astrologically, Yellow Danburite energies are said to complement the zodiac birth signs of Leo. Yellow Danburite energies encompass an element in nature alike fire.

Historically, Yellow Danburite has been known to attract and increase light energies alike the sun to the carrier. Its seldom said that on a rare occasion, one may find a stone that may appear to resemble a materialization of a Buddha formation, just being within it. This is said to be a sign of the light within the stone- reflecting as a metaphor to the wearer of the "enlightenment" to come from within one's self

Metaphysically, Yellow Danburites formation is said to herald energies that will support the student with awakenings and onto spiritual enlightenment. Yellow Danburite instantly feels zesty and energetic to the touch. It boosts energies, but at the same time you can feel the energies coming back into balance and alignment so perfectly and peacefully.

Uses and Purposes

Yellow Danburite these crystals help you by opening your heart fully to the Divine source. You may find yourself becoming more in tune. You may become truly enlightened. Something that is surely needed in these interesting times in which we are living.

Yellow Danburite have a wonderful energy to aid emotional healing. They will also assist you to let go of fear and anxiety, helping you when suffering with grief.

Yellow Danburite worn as jewellery, makes it easier to keep its energy within your auric field during the day.

Yellow Danburite will work with you to clear the pathway you walk upon, bringing the carrier a sense of appreciation for all things and self. Therefore, a strong feeling of self- love will then start to take deep root and blossom within.

Mind, Body & Soul Healing Therapies

Emotional Healing Energy – Yellow Danburite will act as a karmic cleanser, allowing one to transmute and heal the past. Its liberating energies and qualities will support the wearer to let go, giving one the sense of emotional freedom. Yellow Danburite will also enhance the wearer with energies of comfort and clarity. Yellow Danburite is said to boost one's creativity levels, allowing one to become more empowered and consciously creative. Yellow Danburite will enhance one's sense of happiness and attract an abundance of inner joy to the wearer of this particular stone. Yellow Danburite will attract a sense of peace, tranquillity, contentment and love to the carrier of this precious gemstone.

Physical Healing Energy – Yellow Danburite brings energies of vitality and strengths, which means it's an excellent stone to carry if one is suffering from fatigue or exhaustion. It's also known that Yellow Danburite will support and aid one with any skeletal bone conditions or diseases, such as arthritis. Yellow Danburite also works with one as a detoxifying aid, bringing balance back into the body's natural bio rhythms of the endocrine system. Therefore, balancing the distribution and natural flow of chemicals, hormones and energy within. Yellow Danburite is also known to support one's levels of concentration and memory, reducing and regulate stress, anxiety and high blood pressure. It's also known for Danburites energies to assist the bearer, if one faces chronic conditions with their gallbladder or liver. Yellow Danburite also works to aid in reducing allergies.

Chakra Healing Energy - Yellow Danburite acts as an activator, working to stimulate from the Solar Plexus to the Crown chakra energy centre. Although the Danburite gemstone is considered to predominately support the heart centre. I've found that when working with this particular stone, Yellow Danburites energies do encompass the Solar Plexus chakra centre so perfectly and also activates, simulates, bringing one inner vitality and freer flow of energy to this centre included. Ultimately bringing each energy centre in between the Crown and Solar

Plexus chakras, back into alignment. Yellow Danburite is known to carry energies that will assist one with inner healing, cleansing the wearers auric field, while stimulating and drawing one's kundalini energy upwards, restoring and increasing one's natural energy flow. Yellow Danburite is a magnificent stone to mediate with. It will enhance one's energies of awareness, allowing the wearer to become more present and mindful of the stillness within one's meditational space. Yellow Danburite will dispel and un – block any negative energies that may be left laying stagnant in the Solar Plexus and all higher chakras., allowing one to attract more positive energies and connections into one's experiences spiritually. Danburite has been known to assist the spiritual student with receiving and attracting energies, guidance and messages from the etherical realms, such as ancestors, angels, higher astral self and other spirit guides. This particular stone is known to strengthen the connection between the student and source. It's a gemstone enriched with an abundance of enlightenment energies and wisdoms laid within dormant, waiting to be re-woke and claimed. Last but in no way least, Yellow Danburite will completely compliment any angel crystals by enhancing and attracting extra energy unto them.

Activating, Charging, Cleansing & Purifying methods for your Yellow Danburite.

Yellow Danburite can be charged and cleansed by reiki, sage and sun. Moon-light and smudging are the safest options for cleansing all your precious crystals and gemstones.

Yellow Fluorite

 Fluorite is an extremely admired and popular mineral worldwide. Fluorite is formerly known as "Fluorspar". This crystal naturally transpires in all colours, from black, blue, brown, golden champagne, green, pink, purple, red, yellow and violet.

Fluorite has been located in many different areas around the world. Its mineral has been mined in large deposits in many areas, such as Alaska, , Austria Canada, China, Czechoslovakia, England, Germany, Hungary, Kenya, Mexico, New Mexico, Norway, Poland, Switzerland, and within some areas of the United States of America.

Astrologically, Yellow Fluorite energies are said to complement the zodiac birth signs of Aquarius, Capricorn and Pisces. Yellow Fluorite energies encompass elements in nature alike air, water and the planet Neptune.

Historically, Fluorite derived its name from the Latin noun "Fluo", which suggests the flow of water. The French miners name this captivating gem "bleu-jaune", which means blue with a combination of yellow. Therefore, today we all have come to know this gemstone as a "Blue John". Blue John is recognised to attract and expand energies to create a healthy balance between the mind, body and soul

Metaphysically, Yellow Fluorite is said that the brighter these Fluorite stones appear, the brighter one's life shall become, as the energy from this particular crystal, will transform and transmit to the wearer. These energies will enviably encompass one's aura field. Fluorite crystal is known to be amongst the most radiant gemstones in the mineral world.

Uses and Purposes

Yellow Fluorite is a radiant stone alike the sun. It will certainly bring a bright, lighter feeling to your life, as they add a tang and enthusiasm into our lives.

Yellow Fluorite will enhance and attract nurturing energies to the wearer, boosting one's personal growth, allowing one a sense of freedom from fear to explore the world, experiencing the gifts and treasures of what Mother Nature has to give, regarding her as a provider and the most perfect powerful teacher.

Yellow Fluorite is an outstanding learning aid for any student, as Fluorite energies amplify and expands the wearer's ability to concentrate, retaining what has been learnt.

Mind, Body & Soul Healing Therapies

Emotional Healing Energy – Yellow Fluorite will gift the wearer a sense of self-confidence, which will in turn allow the mental and physical tract combined of one, to be brought back into co-ordination and balance.

Yellow Fluorite will deepen one's psychological abilities to think, wisely judging all situations with an open, respectful and considerate mind.

Emotionally, Yellow Fluorite will support the bearer of this particular stone, to ultimately be able to make the right, highest, wisest decisions for themselves and what serves you best.

Yellow Fluorite will bring a sense of calm, contentment, peace and harmony into anyone's life that feels their lives are almost to hectic and chaotic, as Yellow Fluorite will dispel any negative energies surrounding one's auric field. It will transform the negative into positive energies, while working towards harmonizing one's emotions that are teased into the light with this transformation.

Fluorite is also highly celebrated for its ability to balance both right and left hemispheres of one's brain. Therefore, bringing the emotional self-back into alignment, balance and harmony.

Yellow Fluorite will emotionally sooth the wearer, allowing one the freedoms and confidence for oneself, in-order to be able to keep an unbiased opinion over any and all situations.

Physical Healing Energy - Yellow Fluorite is also thought to help with healing of injuries, it can also aid one with skin conditions, and ulcers. It can also assist and aid to strengthen the bone tissue. It's also known to improve and reduce the wearers pains from arthritis, rheumatism, and spinal conditions.

Yellow Fluorite is said to have the energetic ability to alleviate the discomfort caused by cramps, nerval pain and shingles. Yellow Fluorite will enhance and boost one's immune system. This particular crystal will support one with the restructuring and regeneration of the deteriorating cells and DNA.

Yellow Fluorite is known to support one with any respiratory system conditions.

Yellow Fluorite is also known to aid the carrier with breaking old habits, patterns, helping one to guard against indulging in such physical activities.

Chakra Healing Energy - Yellow Fluorite is said to strengthen and increase the flow of life force for the wearer.

Yellow Fluorite is a super - stone, pulling powerful energies towards the Solar Plexus chakra. It has the ability to provide one with a powerful and positive flow of continual energy to this particular chakra, stimulate inner healing, growth and understanding.

Golden fluorite is an exceptionally good stone for the Sacral and Solar Plexus Chakra. All Fluorite crystals, regardless of colour are said to be highly balancing in the energies that are attracted to the Third Eye Chakra. Therefore, Fluorites can increase intuition and psychic abilities, which unites the human mind with the heavenly spirits and divine universal wisdoms.

Yellow Fluorite is considered to clear, cleanse, stabilize and stimulate the aura, allowing one a clearer spiritual connection to the etheric realms. Fluorite, generally known as the "Stone of Discernment", is said to bring onto the physical plane, a higher form of truth, wisdom and unites those perceptions within one's mind, which in turn magically manifests on the material plane.

Fluorite is one of the most powerful and celebrated stones of the "New Age "by spiritual teachers and students. It's known to support and aid ones learning to attain one's desired state of spirituality.

Activating, Charging, Cleansing & Purifying methods for your Yellow Fluorite. Yellow Fluorite can be charged and cleansed by sun, smudging. Moon-light and smudging are the safest options for cleansing all your precious crystals and gemstones.

Yellow Jade

 Jade is said to bless whatever it touches, serving mankind worldwide for nearly 6,000 years. Yellow Jade is one of the rarest types of Jade. It is comprised of magnesium, calcium and Iron silicate. The yellowing of the Jade is caused when ions penetrate and take hoist within the crystal lattice. Yellow Jade colours vary again in shades, from light lemon to deeper golden shades alike the sun.

Jadeite can appear in white-grey green, earthly green, blue or blue-green, emerald green, lavender, pink, red, orange, greenish-black or black. Jadeite is considered much more valuable than Nephrite, although Nephite is known as "the stone of heaven". Jadeite is stronger, rarer, and known to hold higher healing energies.

Nephrite may appear in creamy white, mid- to deep olive green, brown and black. It has a smooth surface polish, with a waxy sheen and is more commonly found.

Jades have been located and mined in countries such as Alaska, China, Japan and the United States of America. Jade is an incredibly durable and tough stone, although its features and texture can change dependant on its origin.

Astrologically, Yellow Jade energies are said to complement the zodiac birth signs of Taurus. Yellow Jade also encompasses element energies of the sun, fire, and the planet Mars in nature.

Historically, Jade is known in China as "Yu". It is the most highly esteemed stone in China throughout recorded history and is extremely valued for its beauty and powers of healing and protection. In the world of science, the name Jade is the name given when two different minerals come together as one - Jade is comprised of Nephrite, a calcium magnesium silicate, and Jadeite, a sodium aluminium silicate. Although they have different compositions, crystal structures, harnesses and densities, both are exceptionally similar in appearance, and thought of as equally valuable in metaphysical properties.

Metaphysically, Yellow Jade is an extremely powerful crystal that will assist one with strengthening their auric field, no matter how successful one becomes, Yellow Jade will always be an ally and attract energies to one that are peaceful, allowing one to remain humble within their own personal power space.

Uses and Purposes

Jades can be carved into incense burners, burial items, vessels, statues, pendants and beads, musical instruments and pieces, that are so delicately inscribed with poetry.

Jade is renowned for its toughness and ability to sharpen and polish, which it a highly sourced stone for weapons, such as knives and axe heads in primitive times.

Jade was used by the people of the British Isles for this particular purpose and by Indigenous tribes of Central and South America, Mexico, and New Zealand. They would cast Jade into wells as an offering to the water spirits for fresh and plentiful water. Many tribes also carved it into ritual artefacts and deity masks. Therefore, one can find an endless variety of treasures carved from Jade.

Mind, Body & Soul Healing Therapies

Emotional Healing Energy – Yellow Jade may also be used to soothe the shock or fear within the very young or very old that must be cared for on an emotional level. This stone brings with it into one's auric field energies of healing, calmness, peace, joy, happiness, wisdom, tranquillity, and optimism.

Yellow Jade will support the bearer of the stone with building one's inner self – esteem, confidence and courage, along with releasing and realising an abundance of inner intelligence and wisdom. Allowing the wearer to rise emotionally from any past traumas into a positive prosperous present.

Yellow Jade placed on the forehead or under the pillow is known to generate insightful dreams. Yellow

Jade Is also known as the stone of "the calm during a storm". It's a dream stone.

Yellow Jade is used in releasing negative thoughts and feelings, thus soothing the mind, bringing peace and clarity to one's senses and emotions. Working with Jade will enhance one's sleep, aiding one to emotionally heal whilst sleeping. This crystal will shine light on dark, past, emotional issues, traumas, and energy blockages, deep from within bringing them to the light for healing and transformation.

Yellow Jade compliments one's aura field with enthusiastic energies, energies of kindness, contentment and thoughtfulness, allowing one to be more mindful and in the present.

Yellow Jade will release the wearer from any forms of judgement, insecurities and depression, leaving the wearer feeling relaxed with a sense of contentment.

Yellow Jade is known to attract to the wearer an abundance positive energy, bringing good fortune to anything you do.

Physical Healing Energy – Yellow Jades energies balance the nerves and soothes one's cardiac rhythm. A piece of Jade kept on one's person will calm and recharge the flow of energy.

Yellow Jade will boost one with healing energies that will assist with enhancing and building one's immunity.

Yellow Jade will improve physical problems related to the bladder, digestive system, heart, blood circulation, larynx, nervous system, spleen, thyroid and thymus. Yellow Jade is also known to simulate and aid one's memory and concentration.

Yellow Jade will boost one's metabolism with an abundance of enriched energies alike the suns, bringing the wearer a sense of vitality and wellbeing, thus dispelling any feeling of fatigue.

Yellow Jade is known to stabilize one's personality, integrating the mind with body to stimulate the flow of energy and ideas, thus making tasks less complex and easier to act upon. Therefore, carrying Yellow Jade will bring energies and a sense of flow and effortlessness, allowing all tasks to seem less physically and mentally draining.

Jades energies supports one to abandon any self-imposed lack, limitations and brings a sense of appreciation and motivation to attain one's ideals and desires.

Yellow Jade will facilitate the energies of ambition, giving one a stronger sense of achievement, allowing one to take the appropriate action when bringing these thoughts into physical reality. Jade is conventionally known to guard one against illness contributes to a longer life span. It's wise to carry a piece always, especially if one is travelling, guarding against any potential foreign diseases one may not have built immunity to.

<u>Chakra Healing Energy</u> - Yellow Jade works to align one's energies, bringing balance into the mind, body and soul combined, to the one that's carrying this certain crystal. Jade will harmonise the Solar Plexus and Heart chakra energy centres, by connecting and combining the flow of energies between the chakras, drawing them both into alignment with one another. Jade is the stone of love. It can elevate the hearts vibrational energies, ultimately to attract love and harmonious relationships into one's life.

Yellow Jade will stimulate and clear any energy blockages within the Solar Plexus, allowing a greater channel and connection to the divine realms.

Spiritually Yellow Jade will support the wearer on all levels of growth, bringing harmony and balance back into being. This crystal can be used when one wishes to master mediation, as Yellow Jade brings a perception of calmness to the soul, allowing one to feel a sense of motionless, which in turn allows one to be more mindful in the moment of nothing within this sacred space. Therefore, allowing one to ease into mediations, becoming the master of their own energy and overall self, mind, body and soul.

<u>Activating, Charging, Cleansing & Purifying methods for your Yellow Jade.</u> This stone can be charged and cleansed by earth, smudging with sage and water. Moon-light and smudging are the safest options for cleansing all your precious crystals and gemstones.

Yellow Jasper

 Yellow Jasper arose from the Old French Jaspre, which means "spotted stone". Jaspers have been admired by ancient cultures and civilizations throughout time until present day. Yellow Jasper is an opaque microcrystalline variety, comprised of a combination of both Chalcedony and Quartz. It's an impure silica with a smooth an opaque transparency. It transpires in nodules, or as fillings in fissures and can be easily sourced. Yellow Jaspers, golden, mustard, or sandy yellow gleaming colouring, is owed to the high iron content, and may contain other impurities or minerals that create luxurious patterns and contours. Yellow Jasper is known to be found within Mookaite Jasper and in Poppy Jasper, in many multi-coloured and orbicular Jaspers.

Jasper has been located and mined in countries such as Australia, Brazil, India, Russia, Uruguay and within some areas of the United States of America.

126

Astrologically, Yellow Jasper energies are said to complement the zodiac birth signs of Leo. Although encompasses an element in nature and energy alike the sun.

Historically, Yellow Jasper was celebrated as a sacred acumen and talisman of protection by priests, shamans and spirit guides, to guard and protect woman and man within both the physical and spiritual journeys. Throughout the Jades are valued stones for their energies and powerful properties of protection they herald. Jaspers have been used multipurpose for these functions they embody, throughout the centuries, for both the physical and spiritual realm.

Metaphysically, Yellow Jasper were known as the "rain bringers", energy nurturers, and healers of the spirit, bringing balance to one's mind, body, and soul. The name that was bestowed upon this stone can be traced as far back, within descriptions in texts of Arabic, Assyrian, Greek, Hebrew, Latin and Persian histories.

Uses and Purposes

Wearing Yellow Jasper for lengthy periods of time allows its energies to assist one with building on self-confidence and enthusiasm, channelling positive energy and attracting others to you.

Yellow Jasper is said to introduce energies of encouragement, enthusiasm and joy, attracting positive friendships and like-minded relationships to the wearer. It's known to support the wearer with building friendships and is said to be favourable for individuals living within small villages and communities, strengthening bonds and relationships

Mind, Body & Soul Healing Therapies

Emotional Healing energy - Yellow Jasper is a marvellous stone, giving great emotional support to the wearer. It draws energies of emotional clarity and will support one into see relationships and situations as they truly are.

128

Yellow Jasper gifts the wearer of the stone a better understanding and perspective of the bigger picture, before one makes a decision with moving forward.

Yellow Jasper is known to provided one with a greater inner mental strength capability, giving one a sense of perseverance to overcome traumatic emotional life experiences. Yellow Jasper will support the wearer with sorting out emotions that are difficult to accept or understand.

Yellow Jaspers energies will encourage the wearer to take the necessary time needed to examine how one truly feels on any issue that's maybe causing one concern in general.

Wear Yellow Jasper to ease chronic worries, stress, anxiety and self-consciousness issues, particularly when it comes down to what others might think or say about you.

Yellow Jasper will ultimately enhance one's ability to increase self-confidence, overcoming any embarrassment, allowing one to set new and stronger boundaries, as well as aid one in looking for realistic and positive solutions and outcomes.

Yellow Jasper is a reliable, yet remarkable stone for rebounding energies of jealousy, as its protective energy makes for a magnificent auric armour, if you are the subject in which the bad energy is aimed at.

Physical Healing Energy - Yellow Jasper is commonly used to build up a stable, long-term immune system. Yellow Jasper is known to aid one with digestion issues. Jasper water can be used to soothe the digestive system and is an extremely enhancing elixir, because it does not over stimulate the bodies energy.

Jasper water is also useful when dealing with problems of the stomach. Alike all elixirs, it can be made by soaking the stone in purified water overnight. Yellow Jasper is also known to assists and regulate the appropriate functioning of the gall bladder, kidneys, liver, pancreas and spleen. It's thought to clear the body of negative energies, such as environmental toxins and impurities.

Yellow Jasper is a great aid, lending emotional support and strength within all areas, boosting physical energy levels, as well as self-discipline. It is thought to soothe bloating, chronic indigestion, fat intolerance and nausea. It's a slow but stabilizing energy, that can deflect negative energy, bringing harmony and balance back within the body.

Yellow Jasper is equally treasured today for those very properties. With this in mind, it's also referred to as the "diet stone". It's gentle but gradual energy vibration assist one to avoid extremes, encouraging patience and perseverance within. Its additionally used as a powerful aid when one needs to fast for long periods of time.

Chakra Healing Energy - Yellow Jasper brings alignment, balance, stability, strength and support to the Solar Plexus chakra. Yellow Jasper connects and aligns the Solar Plexus to the Root chakras energy centre, bringing one a deep sense of connection with the earth's energies.

Yellow Jasper a spectacular stone for grounding and receiving insight in spiritual work, telepathy, astral travel and meditations. Yellow Jasper will provide the Solar Plexus with essential energies, to remove blockages and negative influences from this particular energy centre. Yellow Jasper protects and promotes the flow of energy within this centre.

Yellow Jasper will also assist the free flow of energy within ones Solar Plexus, allowing the distribution between the energies unrestricted freedoms to transmute and create a stronger connection between the lower and higher centres. This certain crystal will enhance the ability to ground one's energies unto the earth with great ease.

Yellow Jaspers "super power", is its ability to transform the energy of the wearer from negative into positive. It's said to have the healing properties of the sun, that will boost one's wellbeing and Solar Plexus energy centre.

Yellow Jasper stimulates the Solar Plexus chakra, bringing to the wearer energies of enthusiasm into one's life, as well as an abundance of sacred knowledge to light, that's been stored deep in the instinctual gut within the Solar Plexus energy centre.

Yellow Jasper has powers to attract only healthy relationships and positive people. The reason for this is Yellow Jasper has a particularly great quality. Its gift to the wearer is the ability to reveal false people, deflecting hate, gossip, jealousy, spite, and all manors of negative energy easily.

Throughout history, Yellow Jasper has been used within meditations to protect and facilitate astral travel, and its effective energies promote dream recall. When using Yellow Jasper, one would place the stone over the chakras, to amplify the universal force of the stone.

Yellow Jasper will re-energize the wearers overall well-being, bringing the harmony and balance between the mind, body and soul. It's a highly conductive stone and will bring to the wearer a deeper sense and connection to all living things.

<u>Activating, Charging, Cleansing & Purifying methods for your Yellow Jasper.</u> can be charged and cleansed by reiki, the sun and sage. Moon-light and smudging are the safest options for cleansing all your precious crystals and gemstones.

Yellow Opal

 The word Opal originates from Sanskrit, meaning "Upala". Priceless gemstone. Opal is a hydrated silica mineral which contains microscopic spheres of silica, which are bound together with water and silica. Yellow Opal is an opaque or translucent yellow, to yellow/ gold or green type of common Opal.

Opal is celebrated for its ability to spread light. Light is comprised of all visible colours, producing an entire spectrum of colours when it is diffracted. As light enters into the opal, it bends around the particles or 'spheres' of hydrated silica, as well as 'chips' of silicon and oxygen suspended within the stone.

Opals have been located in many areas of the world, such as Australia, Brazil, Ethiopia, Indonesia, Japan, Peru, Russia, and within some areas of The United States of America. Although around 90% of the highest quality Opals mined, are sourced from Australia.

Astrologically, Yellow Opal energies are said to complement the zodiac birth signs of Libra. Yellow Opal energies encompasses elements in nature alike fire and water.

Historically, Yellow Opal is renowned for its super-natural power to assist one with developing psychic powers. In ancient Rome times, this particular gemstone was highly sought after, as it was thought to attract energies of love and hope to its carrier. Yellow Opal energies are said to also honour Persephone, the Queen of the underworld.

Metaphysically, Yellow Opal has many magnificent metaphysical properties. Its powerful energy will not only deflect negative energy, but will attract unto the wearer, an abundance of good fortune. Yellow Opal will gift its wearer with a positive approach and outlook towards all life's experiences, past and present, allowing a sunnier future for the one whom carries this particular crystal.

Uses and Purposes

The opal's unique properties were only recently discovered by Australian scientists in the 1960's, with the study of electron microscopes. It was then discovered that small spheres of silica gel caused interference, diffraction and refraction of light, resulting in opal's distinctive show of colour. Yellow Opal is a kaleidoscopic gem, with a combination of colours from Amethyst – purple, Emerald-green, Ruby-red, Sapphire-blue and Topaz- yellow.

Yellow Opal will give you a deeper awareness and insight into how you perceive others, and how they perceive you in return.

Yellow Opal is said to stimulate one's imagination, boosting creativity energy, giving one confidence to come out from their comfort zone

Mind, Body & Soul Healing Therapies

Emotional Healing Energy - Yellow Opal brings with its energies, a feeling to the wearer of joy, happiness, laughter and focus. It will promote a light and fun-loving attitude, helping the wearer to strengthen a sense of self-worth, freedom and independence.

Yellow Opals energy is known to enhance one's emotional ability to reach deeper levels of relaxation, seeing all things from an emotionally stable point of view.

Yellow Opal will also bring up any emotional past energy blockages, as well as any past issues concerning abandonment. Thus, allowing one access to the emotions that are still present and underlaying, needing brought to the surface and light, in-order to be healed.

Ultimately Yellow Opal brings back balance, compassion and alignment, between one's mind, body, and spirit, which will in turn emotional strengthen one's connection to all things.

<u>Physical Healing Energy</u> - Yellow Opal boosts, supports and strengthens the immune system, energizing and assisting the body to become more resistant to infections.

Yellow Opal will bring energy to the wearer that will calm the body and mind, reducing and diminishing stress. Yellow Opals energy will support one with healing with appetite problems, absorption problems, chronic exhaustion, fevers, diabetes, eye issues, kidney, gall stones, infections, insulin regulation, memory, pancreas, and Parkinson's disease.

Yellow Opal will also enhance one's metabolism when feeling run down or exhausted. It's known that Yellow Opal is an extremely magnificent crystal to keep on one's person, in the case of facing any terminal illnesses.

Yellow Opal can help you to recollect and past-life problems associated with one's current physical problems. Yellow Opal is a powerful healing aid, and a tremendous tool when treating souls with neurological conditions. Yellow Opal is said to assist babies that have difficulties when consuming or digesting foods.

<u>Chakra Healing Energy</u> - Yellow Opal supports, connects and enhances the energies of the Solar Plexus as well as the 7th chakra ", The Crown chakra", thus allowing the flow of energies between the Solar Plexus and Crown chakra to be un-blocked, balanced and re-aligned.

Yellow Opal will work as a cleanser, healer, activator and medium for the energy centres, while channelling and connecting one's personal will power of the "Solar Plexus chakra", to the collective power of source the divine the "Crown chakra" connection.

Yellow Opal qualities and energies, alike the sun will stimulate ones Solar Plexus chakra, so that one can have confidence in their thoughts to be able to act accordingly without fear. Yellow Opal is most certainly a stone that will expand one's cosmic consciousness, while strengthening your mystical psychical visions, "telepathy" and divine connection to the etherical realms.

Activating, Charging, Cleansing & Purifying methods for your Yellow Opal. Opal can be charged and cleansed by reiki, smudging with sage, water and sunlight but, to avoid extreme sunlight. Moon-light and smudging are the safest options for cleansing all your precious crystals and gemstones.

Note: The crystals healing meanings are for spiritual healing and support, these are not prescriptions or health care information, or for attaining approval of "Self". When one works towards bestowing "Good Will," putting these actions, feelings, intentions, thoughts and wishes out into the world towards others, and self. Thus, encourages excels one's enlightenment and one's interactions and overall service to humanity.

I would like to give much thanks to ALL reading, for your continued support. If you enjoyed this book? I would like to invite you!!, to continue reading my collection of books.

I would like to wish you all the very best, along with my love & light for the journey ahead and remember that! Nothing can dim the "Divine, Eternal Light & Love" that shines from deep within you. These gemstones are tools, to complement and enhance one's energies ONLY, the real change comes from within, Ase.

Additional Universal You Books

- Crystals & Precious Gemstones – For the Root Chakra Energy Centre.

Michelle Janet Summers
Universal You Crystals & Precious Gemstones: Root Chakra

- Crystals & Precious Gemstones – For the Sacral Chakra Energy Centre.

Michelle Summers
Universal You Crystals & Precious Gemstones: Sacral Chakra

- Crystals & Precious Gemstones – For the Heart Chakra Energy Centre.

- Crystals & Precious Gemstones – For the Throat Chakra Energy Centre.

- Crystals & Precious Gemstones – For the Third-Eye Chakra Energy Centre.

- Crystals & Precious Gemstones – For the Crown Chakra Energy Centre.

Affirmation Books:
- Chakra Energy Cleansing & Activating Affirmations

Michelle Summers
Universal You Chakra Healing Affirmations
★★★★★ (1)

- Life, Love & Light Affirmations

Michelle Summers
Universal You Life, Love & Light Affirmations

Universal You Life, Love &
Light Affirmations

Thank you for reading.... Blessings

Love & Light as you go!!

from myself, Mj-Summers.

OXOXOX

Michelle J Summers   @Universal You.

All my love light, blessings
be with you all 2020
& beyond
x x x

Bill

Printed in Poland
by Amazon Fulfillment
Poland Sp. z o.o., Wrocław

61601281R00086